MY KETO

Complete Ketogenic Diet for Beginners: Living the Keto Lifestyle

BY

MAYA ROGERS

Contents

INTRODUCTION

If you've followed eating patterns lately, you've likely known about the ketogenic keto diet. This high-fat, low-carb technique for eating has spellbound mainstream society, and more individuals than any time in recent memory are pondering whether it will have any kind of effect for their wellbeing. For the following a month, we will distill the realities about the ketogenic keto diet into a progression of articles so you can leave away with a superior comprehension of what this eating routine guarantees and whether it bodes well for you.

For this first article, we're going to take a gander at the historical backdrop of this regularly misjudged keto diet and track its ascent in fame today. You will be amazed to know that the purposefully entering ketosis isn't new; however, instead owes its motivation to notable epilepsy inquire about finished just about a century back.

The Basics of Ketosis

At an essential level, the ketogenic keto diet is established in the possibility that restricting your sugar admission and devouring fats instead will place your body in a "fasted state" where it will consume ketones rather than glucose-bringing about better wellbeing for you.

The focal thought is that following a feast plan of 60-75% fat, 15-30% protein, and 5-10% carbs place the body in a state called ketosis. While your framework essentially decides to run on glucose (sugar), limiting your starch admission will make it feel that it's destitute, so it will produce an optional vitality source from fat to keep sending glucose to the mind. At the point when you limit your carb supply, your body begins to separate fat into mixes called ketones, which are an elective fuel source that numerous individuals accept has unique advantages for your wellbeing and weight.

KOREAN BRAISED TOFU

Cook Time: 10 minutes

Servings: 4

Ingredients:

- 14 oz. block firm tofu, cut into 16 squares
- 1 tablespoon sugar
- 1 scallion, thinly cut
- 1 onion, thinly cut
- 3 tablespoons soy sauce
- 1 tablespoon Korean chili powder
- 4 tablespoons sake

- Sesame seeds, toasted

Instructions:

1. Add onion slices in a pan and add tofu on top. Mix soy sauce, Korean chili powder, sake, and sugar in a bowl and add over tofu slices.

2. Cover pan. Increase heat to high and cook until it boils. Turn heat to medium-high and cook for 5 minutes, baste with sauce.

3. Remove lid, increase heat to high and cook until sauce reduces.

4. Transfer to a plate, garnish with sesame seeds and serve.

RED LENTIL TIKKA MASALA

Cook Time: 30 minutes

Servings: 5

Ingredients:

- 1 onion, diced
- 2 tablespoons olive oil
- 3 garlic cloves, minced
- 1 jalapeno pepper, minced
- 1 tablespoon ginger, grated
- 1 ½ tablespoons garam masala
- 1 tablespoon tomato paste
- 1 tablespoon coconut sugar
- 28 oz can tomatoes, crushed
- 1 cup red lentils
- 1 ½ cups vegetable broth
- ½ cup of coconut milk
- ¼ cup cilantro, chopped
- Salt and pepper, to taste

Instructions:

1. Cook onions and jalapeno pepper in hot olive oil in a pan until soft. Add garam masala, garlic, ginger, and tomato paste and stir for 1 minute.

2. Add coconut sugar, tomatoes, and vegetable broth. Mix well and add red lentils.

3. Bring to a simmer, turn the heat down and cook for about 30 minutes.

4. Add cilantro and coconut milk and mix. Serve and enjoy.

EASY THAI RED TOFU CURRY

Cook Time: 30 minutes

Servings: 4

Ingredients:

- 16 oz. tofu, pressed and cut into ½" cubes
- 4 garlic clove, minced
- 2 tablespoons sesame oil
- 4 tablespoons soy sauce
- 3 tablespoons rice vinegar
- 1 tablespoon brown sugar
- 1 teaspoon red pepper flakes
- 3 tablespoons corn starch

- 1 yellow onion, minced
- 1 teaspoon ginger, grated
- 1 red bell pepper, sliced
- 1 cup Cremini mushrooms, sliced
- 3 tablespoons red curry paste
- 13 oz. coconut milk
- 1 tablespoon sambal oelek
- 1 lime, zest and juice
- 8 Thai basil leaves, ribboned
- Cooked rice

Instructions:

1. Drain and press the tofu for 30 minutes. Mix 1 garlic clove, 3 tablespoons soy sauce, 2 tablespoons sesame oil, 1 tablespoon brown sugar, rice vinegar, red pepper flakes and corn starch in a bowl.

2. Cut tofu into cubes and add to the freezer bag, add the marinade and refrigerate for 30 minutes. Transfer tofu to a bowl and add cornstarch. Mix well.

3. Heat coconut oil in a pan over medium heat. Fry tofu cubes for 2 minutes on each side. Transfer to a bowl.

4. Add ¼ cup water to the pan and bring to a simmer. Add garlic, ginger and minced onion and turn the heat to medium. Cook for 5 minutes. Add mushrooms and red bell pepper. Add 3 tablespoons red curry paste and mix well.

5. Add coconut milk, lime juice and zest and soy sauce. Mix well and cook for 15 minutes.

6. Serve with rice.

BARBECUE BAKED SEITAN STRIPS

Cook time: 1 hour

Servings: 4

Ingredients:

- ½ cup nutritional yeast
- 3 cups vital wheat gluten
- 1 ½ teaspoon smoked paprika
- 1 ½ tablespoon garlic powder
- 1 teaspoon onion powder
- ½ teaspoon dried oregano
- ½ teaspoon dried basil
- 3 ½ cups vegetable broth
- 2 cups vegan barbecue sauce
- 5 tablespoons olive oil
- 5 tablespoons maple syrup
- 3 tablespoons soy sauce
- 1 teaspoon liquid smoke
- 1 teaspoon garlic powder
- 1 ½ teaspoons black pepper

Instructions:

1. Preheat the oven to 390F.
2. Mix gluten, yeast, 1 ½ tablespoon garlic powder, 1 teaspoon smoked paprika, 1 teaspoon onion powder, ½ teaspoon black pepper, ½ teaspoon oregano and ½ teaspoon basil in a bowl.

3. Mix 1 cup BBQ sauce, 2 tablespoons maple syrup, 1 ½ cups vegetable broth, 2 tablespoons olive oil and 1 tablespoon soy sauce in a bowl. Add liquid to dry ingredients and mix well. Knead the mixture until the dough is formed. Let rest.

4. Mix the remaining broth, BBQ sauce, maple syrup, olive oil, soy sauce, liquid smoke, black pepper, garlic powder, and smoked paprika in a bowl and mix well to make a marinade.

5. Place dough on a flat surface and flatten. Add a little oil and roll out to 1" thick and rectangle shape. Add 1 cup marinade to a tray and place dough on top. Cover with the remaining marinade. Bake for 1 hour adds 1 cup broth if it dries in between.

6. Serve and enjoy.

TERIYAKI GLAZED TOFU STEAKS

Cook Time: 15 minutes

Servings: 3

Ingredients:

- 14 oz. block tofu
- 1 teaspoon garlic, minced
- 1/2 teaspoon ginger, grated
- 1 tablespoon lemon juice
- 4 tablespoons soy sauce
- 2 tablespoons maple syrup
- 1 tablespoon rice vinegar
- 1/4 teaspoon corn starch
- 1/4 teaspoon Dijon mustard

- Oil

Instructions:

1. Mix all ingredients except oil and tofu in a bowl to make the sauce. Cut tofu into 1/2" thick slices.

2. Coat a pan with oil and heat over medium-high. Add the tofu steaks. Flip and cook until crust is brown from all sides. Leave last batch in pan and add half of teriyaki sauce.

3. Coat the tofu steaks thoroughly with the sauce and cook for 2 minutes. Repeat with the remaining tofu steaks and sauce. Serve and enjoy.

EASY VEGAN CHILLI SIN CARNE

Cook Time: 40 minutes

Servings: 6

Ingredients:

- 3 garlic cloves, minced
- 2 tablespoon olive oil
- 2 celery stalks, chopped
- 1 red onion, sliced
- 2 red peppers, chopped
- 2 carrots, peeled and chopped
- 1 teaspoon chili powder
- 1 teaspoon ground cumin
- 1 lb canned tomatoes, chopped
- 14 oz can red kidney beans, drained and rinsed
- 3 1/2 oz split red lentils
- 14 oz frozen soy mince
- 1 cup vegetable stock
- salt and pepper, to taste
- basmati rice, cooked

Instructions:

1. Heat olive oil in a pan. Cook carrots, onion, celery, garlic and peppers over medium heat until softened. Add chili powder, cumin and salt and pepper and mix well to combine.
2. Add kidney beans. lentils, chopped tomatoes, vegetable stock and soy mince. Cook for about 25 minutes, stirring often.
3. Serve with basmati rice.

TERIYAKI TOFU STIR FRY OVER QUINOA

Cook Time: 30 minutes

Servings: 4

Ingredients:

- 1 lb. asparagus
- 14 oz. firm tofu
- 2 tablespoon green onions, chopped
- 4 tablespoon tamari
- 2 teaspoon cooking oil
- 1 tablespoon sesame oil
- 5 garlic cloves, minced
- 1 1/2 tablespoon rice vinegar

- 1/2 tablespoon ginger, grated
- 1/4 cup coconut sugar
- 1/2 cup water
- 2 teaspoon cornstarch
- 4 cups quinoa, cooked

Instructions:

1. Cut tofu block in half. Squeeze to remove excess liquid. Cut into 1/2" thick cubes and fry in 1 teaspoon cooking oil on medium-high heat until lightly brown on all sides. Add 1 tablespoon tamari and toss. Set aside.

2. Mix 3 tablespoon tamari, sesame oil, rice vinegar, garlic cloves, ginger, coconut sugar, corn starch and water in a bowl for sauce. Cut asparagus into 2" long pieces and dice other veggies.

3. Heat 1 teaspoon cooking oil in a pan over medium-high heat. Cook diced veggies until crispy. Add in the tofu. Add in the sauce. Lower heat and cook until sauce thickens.

4. Turn off heat and add over the cooked quinoa. Serve and enjoy.

LENTILS WITH BROCCOLI RABE

Cook time: 50 minutes

Servings: 4

Ingredients:

- 1 onion, chopped
- 1 garlic clove, minced
- 4 tablespoons olive oil
- 1 tablespoon tomato paste
- 1 ½ cups French lentils
- 3 cups vegetable stock
- 1 bunch broccoli rabe
- 1 garlic clove, sliced
- 1 tomato, chopped
- 2 tablespoons butter
- ½ cup heavy cream
- Handful basil leaves, torn
- Salt and pepper, to taste

Instructions:

1. Heat 2 tablespoon olive oil in a pan. Cook onions for 8 minutes over low heat and season to taste.

2. Add minced garlic and cook for 1 minute more. Add tomato paste, lentils, and a splash of stock. Turn the heat to medium and cook until the stock is absorbed. Add the rest of the stock and cook for 30 minutes.

3. Bring a pot of water to a boil. Add broccoli rabe and cook for 2 minutes. Remove and add to an ice bath to cool down. Drain.

4. Heat the remaining oil in a pan. Add broccoli rabe and garlic cloves — season and cook for 3 minutes.

5. Add chopped tomato to the lentils and cook for 3 minutes. Add the butter and cream. Add basil leaves, add sautéed broccoli rabe on top and serve.

CAESAR WHITE BEAN BURGERS

Cook time: 20 minutes

Servings: 4

Ingredients:

- 2 (14 oz) cans white beans, rinsed and drained
- ½ onion, diced
- 2 tablespoons olive oil
- 2 garlic cloves, minced
- 1/3 cup vegan Parmesan cheese, shredded
- ½ cup breadcrumbs
- 1 flax egg
- ¼ cup parsley leaves, chopped
- 1 tablespoon anchovy paste
- 3 tablespoons lemon juice

- 2 teaspoons Dijon mustard
- 2 teaspoons Worcestershire sauce
- 4 hamburger buns
- ¼ teaspoon salt and pepper

Instructions:

1. Heat 1 tablespoon oil in a pan over medium heat. Add the onion and cook for about 3-4 minutes. Add garlic and cook for 1 minute more. Remove the pan from heat.
2. Blend beans in a blender until broken down. Add onion, breadcrumbs, parsley, vegan cheese, flax egg, lemon juice, Worcestershire, anchovy paste, mustard, salt, and pepper to the bowl and mix well to combine. Cover and refrigerate for 2 hours.
3. Divide the mixture into 4 parts and shape each one into ½" patty.
4. Heat the remaining oil in a pan over medium heat. Add the patties. Cook for 6 minutes flip and cook the other side for 6 minutes. Place patties on the buns and serve.

SOUTHWESTERN QUINOA STUFFED PEPPERS

Cook time: 30 minutes

Servings: 8

Ingredients:

- 1 tablespoon olive oil
- 1 cup quinoa, rinsed
- 1 yellow onion, diced
- 2 tablespoons tomato paste
- 1 ½ teaspoon chili powder
- 1 ½ teaspoon ground cumin
- 2 garlic cloves, chopped
- 2 cups of water
- 8 red bell peppers
- 15 oz. can black beans, drained and rinsed
- ½ cup cilantro, chopped
- 1 ½ cups corn kernels
- 1 teaspoon salt
- Black pepper, to taste

Instructions:

1. Heat the oven to 375F and place a rack in the middle. Add 1 cup of water to the baking dish and set aside.

2. Heat 1 tablespoon oil in a pan over medium heat. Add onion, season to taste, and cook for 8 minutes.

3. Add quinoa and cook for 2 minutes. Add garlic, chili powder, tomato paste, and cumin and cook for 2 minutes. Add 2 cups water and one teaspoon salt and mix well. Bring everything to a boil. Reduce the heat to low, cover and cook for 15 minutes.

4. Cut a circle around each bell pepper stem. Remove any seeds and membranes from it. Drizzle each one with oil and season with salt and pepper and set aside.

5. Let quinoa stand for 5 minutes once done. Fluff with a fork add cilantro, beans, and corns and stir well — season with salt and pepper.

6. Divide the mixture among peppers. Top with the caps. Transfer the stuffed peppers into the baking dish. Cover tightly with foil.

7. Bake for 1 hour. Let rest for 5 minutes. Serve and enjoy.

TOFU CHICKPEA STIR-FRY WITH TAHINI SAUCE

Cook time: 15 minutes

Servings: 4

Ingredients:

- ¼ cup tahini
- 2 tablespoons soy sauce
- 2 teaspoons honey
- 1/3 cup water
- 1 teaspoon ginger, minced
- 2 tablespoons rice vinegar
- 1 cup cooked chickpeas, drained and rinsed
- 1 tablespoon peanut oil
- ½ red onion, sliced
- 2 teaspoons ginger, chopped
- 1 red bell pepper, cored, seeded and diced
- 8 oz baked tofu, cubed
- 4 cups cooked rice
- Sesame seeds, toasted
- Minced chives

Instructions:

1. Mix the first 6 ingredients to make the sauce and place near the stove.

2. Preheat oil in a skillet over medium heat. Add chickpeas and cook for about 2 minutes. Add the ginger and cook for 1 minute more.

3. Add peppers and onions and cook for 3 minutes. Add baked tofu and cook for 5 minutes.

4. Add tahini sauce over tofu and cook the mixture for 1 minute. Add to the cooked rice, sprinkle with sesame seeds and top with minced chives.

5. Serve and enjoy.

SMOKY TEMPEH BURRITO BOWLS

Cook Time: 1 hour 45 minutes

Servings: 3

Ingredients:

- 15 oz. can black beans
- ½ teaspoon cumin powder
- 1 cup uncooked brown rice
- Water
- 10 oz. tempeh
- 1 tablespoon avocado oil
- ½ white onion, diced
- 1 tablespoon olive oil

- 2 garlic cloves, minced
- 15 oz. tomato sauce
- 1 whole chipotle in adobo sauce
- 1 tablespoon adobo sauce
- Red cabbage, sliced

Instructions:

1. Add 1" water to a saucepan and bring to a simmer. Add the steamer basket on top and add tempeh to the basket. Steam for 15 minutes. Cube and set aside.
2. Heat a skillet over medium heat. Add oil and onion. Cook for 3 minutes add garlic and cook for 2 minutes.
3. Add chipotle pepper, adobo sauce, and tomato sauce and mix. Heat until starts to bubble, reduce the heat and simmer for 4 minutes.
4. Transfer the sauce to a blender and blend on high until smooth. Transfer the sauce back to the skillet and heat over low heat.
5. Add the black beans to a pan and heat over medium heat. Once boils, reduce the heat, add cumin, and add salt.
6. Heat a skillet over medium heat. Add oil and cubed steamed tempeh and cook for 8 minutes until crisp. Add to the red sauce and mix well. Cover with the lid for 3 minutes, remove and simmer over low heat.
7. Divide everything among 4 serving bowls. Add red cabbage.
8. Serve and enjoy.

SWEET AND SOUR TEMPEH

Cook time: 20 minutes

Servings: 2

Ingredients:

- 1 brown onion
- 1 packet tempeh, gluten-free
- 1 teaspoon sesame oil
- 1 tablespoon sunflower oil
- ½ bell pepper
- 1/3 cup rice vinegar
- 1 tablespoon ketchup
- 4 tablespoons coconut sugar
- 1 teaspoon tamari
- 2 teaspoons cornstarch
- 4 teaspoons water
- Handful of snow peas

Instructions:

1. Dissolve cornstarch in water.
2. Mix rice vinegar, ketchup, coconut sugar and tamari in a pan placed over medium heat. Bring to a boil. Remove from heat, add cornstarch mixture, and set aside.
3. Cut tempeh into squares. Cut bell peppers into slices and prepare the snow peas. Add sesame and sunflower oil into a pan. Fry tempeh until brown.

4. Dice onion and add to the tempeh and cook until browned. Add prepped veggies and cook for about 3 minutes. Add the sauce, mix well to coat well, and cook for 2 minutes.

5. Serve and enjoy.

VEGAN FALL FARRO PROTEIN BOWL

Cook Time: 45 minutes

Servings: 2

Ingredients:

- 1 cup carrots, diced
- 1 cup sweet potatoes, diced
- 15 oz. can chickpeas, drained and rinsed
- 1 1/2 cups water
- 2 teaspoons cooking oil
- 4 oz. smoky tempeh strips
- 1/2 cup farro, uncooked
- 2 cups mixed greens
- 2 tablespoon almonds, roasted
- 1/4 cup hummus
- 4 lemon wedges
- salt and pepper, to taste

Instructions:

1. Preheat the oven to 375F and prepare a baking sheet.
2. Mix carrots and sweet potatoes with 1 teaspoon cooking oil and salt and pepper in a bowl. Spread on one half of the baking sheet.
3. Mix chickpeas, remaining oil, 1/8 teaspoon black pepper and pinch salt in a bowl. Spread on the second half of the baking sheet.

4. Add tempeh strips on the baking sheet and roast all for 30 minutes. Flip and shuffle everything at half point. Add farro grains, water, and pinch of salt to a pot and place over medium heat. Cover, bring to a boil and reduce the heat and cook for 25 minutes. Divide farro, greens, and roasted tempeh, chickpeas, and potatoes among 4 bowls. Top with wedges, almonds, and hummus. Serve and enjoy.

BLACK BEAN AND QUINOA BALLS AND SPIRALIZED ZUCCHINI

Cook time: 55 minutes

Servings: 4

Ingredients:

- 4 zucchinis
- 1/4 cup sesame seeds
- 1 can black beans
- 1/2 cup quinoa
- 2 tablespoon tomato paste
- 1/4 cup oat flour
- 1/2 tablespoon Sriracha
- 2 tablespoon nutritional yeast
- 1 teaspoon garlic powder
- 1 1/2 tablespoon herbs, chopped
- 1 tablespoon apple cider vinegar
- 1 cup cherry tomatoes, halved
- 1/2 cup sun-dried tomatoes
- 1 garlic clove
- 2 tablespoon pine nuts, toasted
- 2 tablespoon nutritional yeast
- 1 teaspoon oregano
- A handful basil
- salt and pepper, to taste

Instructions:

1. Add 1 cup water and quinoa to a pot and cook for about 15 minutes. Drain water and let cool. Add black beans to a bowl and mash with a fork.

2. Add sesame seeds, quinoa, oat flour, Sriracha, yeast, tomato paste and spices and mix well. Shape the mixture into balls. Place on a lined baking sheet.

3. Bake at 400 F for 40 minutes.

4. Add 1/2 cup cherry tomatoes, sun-dried tomatoes, apple cider vinegar, garlic clove, pine nuts, yeast, basil, oregano and salt and pepper to a blender and blend until creamy to make the sauce.

5. Spiralize zucchinis and add to a bowl. Add tomato sauce and 1/2 cup cherry tomatoes to the bowl and add 5 quinoa balls per serving. Serve and enjoy!

MONGOLIAN SEITAN
(VEGAN MONGOLIAN BEEF)

Cook Time: 30 minutes

Servings: 6

Ingredients:

- 2 tablespoon + 2 teaspoon vegetable oil
- 3 garlic cloves, minced
- 1/2 teaspoon ginger, minced
- 1/3 teaspoon red pepper flakes
- 1/2 cup soy sauce
- 2 teaspoons corn starch
- 2 tablespoons cold water

- 1/2 cup + 2 tablespoons coconut sugar
- 1 lb homemade seitan
- Rice, cooked, for serving

Instructions:

1. Heat 2 teaspoons vegetable oil in a pan over medium heat. Add garlic and ginger and mix well. Add red pepper flakes after 30 seconds and cook for 1 minute.

2. Add coconut sugar and soy sauce and mix well. Reduce the heat to medium-low and cook for 7 minutes. Mix cornstarch and water and add to the pan and mix well to combine. Cook for 3 minutes reduce the heat to lowest and simmer.

3. Heat the remaining oil in a skillet over medium-high heat. Add the seitan and cook for 5 minutes.

4. Reduce the heat and add the sauce to the pan. Mix well to coat every seitan piece and cook until all sauce adheres. Remove from heat.

5. Serve with rice.

TERIYAKI TEMPEH

Cook Time: 40 minutes

Servings: 4

Ingredients:

- 1 tablespoon olive oil
- 8 oz. organic tempeh
- 5 tablespoon tamari
- 3 tablespoon vegetable broth
- 1/4 teaspoon onion powder
- 1 teaspoon garlic powder
- 1 teaspoon sesame oil
- 2 tablespoon maple syrup
- 1 teaspoon apple cider vinegar
- 1 teaspoon sriracha
- 1/2 teaspoon cornstarch
- sesame seeds

Instructions:

1. Cut tempeh into triangles and steam for 10 minutes. Add vegetable broth, 1 tablespoon tamari, 1/2 teaspoon garlic powder and onion powder in a bowl and mix well to combine. Pour marinade over tempeh. Let rest for 20 minutes

2. Add olive oil to the pan and cook tempeh for 4 minutes per side. Mix the remaining tamari, sesame oil, maple syrup, sriracha,

apple cider vinegar, remaining garlic powder and cornstarch in a bowl.

3. Add cooked tempeh to this sauce and mix well. Add covered tempeh back to the pan. Heat for 30 seconds per side turn the heat off and add the remaining sauce into the pan. Let rest for 1 minute.

4. Top with sesame seeds and serve.

VEGAN SPINACH RICOTTA LASAGNA

Cook Time: 1 hour 10 minutes

Servings: 4

Ingredients:

- 1 lb firm tofu
- 2 tablespoons olive oil
- 5 garlic cloves
- 1 tablespoon mustard
- 2 lemons, juiced
- 1 teaspoon salt
- A pinch nutmeg
- A pinch black pepper
- 1/3 cup margarine
- 1/3 cup flour
- 3 cup soy sauce
- 2 teaspoon dried oregano
- 3/4 cup passata
- 1 lb frozen spinach, 2/3 lb lasagna sheets

Instructions:

1. Defrost the spinach. Add olive oil, garlic cloves, lemon juice, nutmeg, mustard, black pepper and 1/2 teaspoon salt to a blender and blend until smooth. Break the tofu into chunks and add to the blender. Blend until crumbly. Melt margarine in a pan, add flour and mix well. Add soy milk and 1/2 teaspoon salt and keep

whisking.   Mix passata, dried oregano, salt, and pepper in a bowl. Prepare lasagne by starting with a layer of lasagna noodles and top with the tofu mixture. Next top with the sauce. Top last lasagne sheet with both sauces to fully cover the pasta. Bake for 40 minutes at 375 F. Serve and enjoy.

VEGAN SAMOSA PIE

Cook Time: 35 minutes

Servings: 4

Ingredients:

- 3 tablespoon vegetable oil
- 1 onion, diced
- 2 potatoes, peeled and diced
- 1 cup frozen green peas
- 3 garlic cloves, minced
- 9/10 lb. frozen soy mince
- 1 tablespoon dried coriander
- 2 tablespoon curry powder
- 1 teaspoon chili powder
- 1 pack filo pastry
- Salt and pepper, to taste

Instructions:

1. Preheat the oven to 350F and let filo pastry come to room temperature.
2. Cook potatoes in boiling water in a pot until soft. Drain and mash.
3. Heat oil in a pan and cook garlic and onion until soft. Add coriander, curry powder and chili powder and cook for 1 minute then add soy mince. Add 1 drop water and cook for 10 minutes on medium heat.

4. Mix mash mixture with soy mince and season with salt and pepper. Transfer to a baking dish and smooth in one layer. Layer filo pastry on top of the mince mixture, one sheet at a time and use oil to grease. Slice 4 slits on top.

5. Cook in the oven for 20 minutes. Serve and enjoy.

BLACK BEAN CHOCOLATE ORANGE MOUSSE

Cook time: 10 minutes + chilling time

Servings: 6

Ingredients:

- 2 tablespoons coconut oil, melted
- 8 tablespoons brown rice
- 15 oz. can black beans, drained and rinsed
- 1 7/10 oz. pitted dates
- 5 tablespoons cacao powder
- 1 orange zest
- 4 tablespoons milk, non-dairy
- 1 teaspoon cacao nibs

Instructions:

1. Add black beans and dates to a blender and blend on high for 1 minute. Add the brown rice syrup, coconut oil, milk and cacao powder and blend for 1 minute until smooth.
2. Add in the orange zest. Transfer the mixture to 6 espresso cups, add cacao nibs and little orange zest.
3. Place into the refrigerator until ready and serve.

CHOCOLATE CRISPY FRUIT SQUARES

Cook time: 10 minutes + chilling time

Servings: 9-12 squares

Ingredients:

- 1 cup raisins
- 1 cup dates
- 2 tablespoons sesame seeds
- 1/2 cup walnuts, chopped
- 1/4 cup dark chocolate chips, dairy-free
- 1 cup of rice cereal, puffed

Instructions:

1. Blend raisins and dates in a blender for 30 seconds. Add sesame seeds and walnuts and blend for 20 seconds. Add chocolate chips and cereal. Mix well to combine.
2. Transfer the mixture to a glass dish and press it into the bottom of the dish. Cover and refrigerate for 1 hour.
3. Cut into square bars and serve.

FLOURLESS SALTED CARAMEL CHOCOLATE CHIP COOKIES

Cook Time: 15 minutes

Servings: 8 cookies

Ingredients:

- 5 Medjool dates, pits removed
- 1 cup cashew butter
- 2 tablespoon water
- 1 teaspoon vanilla extract
- 1/4 teaspoon baking powder
- 1/4 cup dark chocolate chips
- 1/4 teaspoon sea salt

Instructions:

1. Preheat the oven to 350 F and soak dates in water for 30 minutes and drain the dates.

2. Mix sea salt, dates, 2 tablespoon water in a blender and blitz until caramel forms. Remove.

3. Mix vanilla, baking powder and cashew butter in the blender. Add caramel to this mixture and pulse to combine. Add chocolate chips and pulse well.

4. Transfer to a parchment paper lined baking sheet. Bake for about 10 minutes. Let cool and remove. Serve and enjoy!

MANGO CHIA SEED PUDDING

Cook Time: 10 minutes

Servings: 4

Ingredients:

- 1/2 cup chia seeds
- 2 cups of coconut milk
- 1 teaspoon vanilla extract
- 2 mangoes
- 1/4 teaspoon cardamom
- 3 tablespoon coconut nectar

Instructions:

1. Add chia seeds, vanilla, cardamom, coconut milk, and coconut nectar into a bowl and mix well. Stir well, cover, and refrigerate.
2. Place the mango upright and slice right and left side vertically so that the center remains. Slice the sides and discard the stones.
3. Push mango skin inside and cut into crisscross grids. Run knife beneath the grid to separate the flesh from skin.
4. Blend the mango in a blender until pureed puree.
5. Mix mango and chia seeds and serve.

BANANA BREAD COOKIES

Cook Time: 25 minutes

Servings: 18

Ingredients:

- 2 tablespoon maple syrup
- 2 ripe bananas
- 1/2 cup peanut butter
- 2 cups quick-cook oats
- 1 tablespoon chia seeds
- 1 teaspoon cinnamon
- 1/4 cup mini chocolate chips
- 1/2 teaspoon salt
- A dash nutmeg

Instructions:

1. Preheat the oven to 350F.
2. Mash bananas in a bowl and add maple syrup and peanut butter. Mix well.
3. Add chia seeds, oats, cinnamon and nutmeg and mix well. Add the chocolate chips.
4. Shape the batter into the balls and place on the baking sheet, Flatten with a spoon and bake for 15 minutes.
5. Serve and enjoy.

SIMPLE BAKED CHEESECAKE

Cook time: 45 minutes

Servings: 6-8

Ingredients:

- 8 Medjool dates pitted
- 1 1/2 cup cashews
- 2 tablespoon cashew butter
- 1 cup vanilla coconut yogurt
- 1 cup raw cashews, presoaked and drained
- 1 lemon juice
- 6 tablespoon agave
- 1 teaspoon vanilla extract
- 1 tablespoon psyllium husk
- 1/2 teaspoon raw ground vanilla bean
- 1 teaspoon salt

Instructions:

1. Preheat the oven to 350F and oil a springform pan and set aside.
2. Blend 1 1/2 cup cashews, dates and cashew butter in a blender until a crumble forms. Transfer to the oiled pan and press down to shape a crust. Set aside.
3. Blend the rest of the ingredients until very smooth. Add over the crust. Bake in a preheated oven for 45 minutes remove and cool completely.
4. Slice and serve.

GLUTEN-FREE PEAR AND BANANA LOAF

Cook time: 45 minutes

Servings: 1 loaf

Ingredients:

- 3/4 cup oat flour
- 3/4 cup chickpea flour
- 2 teaspoons baking powder
- 3/4 teaspoon baking soda
- 3/4 cup almond meal
- 1/2 teaspoon ground cinnamon
- 1 1/2 cups ripe pears, peeled, chopped and divided
- 3/4 cup ripe banana, sliced
- 1 tablespoon lemon juice
- 6 tablespoons maple syrup
- 1 1/2 teaspoon vanilla extract
- 1/4 teaspoon salt

Instructions:

1. Preheat the oven to 350F and line a loaf pan with parchment paper.
2. Mix oat flour, almond meal, chickpea flour, cinnamon, baking soda, baking powder, and salt and set aside.
3. Blend 3/4 cup chopped pear, maple syrup, lemon juice, banana, and vanilla until smooth. Transfer the mixture to the dry ingredients and mix. Add the remaining chopped pears.

4. Transfer the batter to the prepared pan and spread evenly — Bake for 45 minutes.

5. Let fresh, slice and serve.

PLANT-BASED BLUEBERRY CRISP

Cook Time: 55 minutes

Servings: 12

Ingredients:

- 2 cups oats
- 7 cups blueberries
- 1 cup maple syrup
- 1 lemon, juiced and zested
- 1 cup almonds, sliced
- 2 tablespoons flax seeds
- 1/2 cup water
- 4 tablespoons cinnamon
- 1 1/2 teaspoons salt

Instructions:

1. Preheat the oven to 375F.
2. Add blueberries to a baking dish. Squeeze lemon juice over them. Blend 1 cup oats, flax seeds, 1/2 cup almonds, 2 tablespoon cinnamon and 1 teaspoon salt.
3. Add 1 cup oats, 1/2 teaspoon salt, 1/2 cup almonds, 1/2 lemon zest, 1/4 cup water and 1/2 cup maple syrup in a bowl and mix.
4. Add the remaining maple syrup over the berries. Add blended oat mixture, wet oat mixture, 1/4 cup water, remaining lemon zest and 2 tablespoon cinnamon in this order over the berries.
5. Bake for 35 minutes. Serve and enjoy.

PLANT-BASED PEANUT BUTTER CREAM SWEET POTATO BROWNIES

Cook Time: 60 minutes

Servings: 10

Ingredients:

- 2 sweet potatoes
- 1/4 cup + 3 tablespoon peanut butter
- 8 dates, soaked and pitted
- 4 tablespoons maple syrup
- 8 oz. coconut cream, chilled
- 1/4 cup cacao
- A pinch cinnamon

Instructions:

1. Microwave the sweet potatoes until tender. Blend cooked sweet potato (without skin), 1/4 cup peanut butter, dates, 2 tablespoon maple syrup and cacao in a blender.

2. Transfer to a muffin tin leaving space in the middle. Bake on 325 F for 30 minutes. Let cool.

3. Whip cooled coconut cream, remaining syrup and peanut butter. Fill brownies with filling.

4. Sprinkle with cinnamon. Let cool overnight in the fridge and serve.

RAW CHICKPEA COOKIE DOUGH

Cook Time: 10 minutes

Servings: 2

Ingredients:

- 1 tablespoon vanilla extract
- 1 can chickpeas, drained and rinsed
- 1 tablespoon peanut butter
- 3 tablespoon maple syrup
- 1/4 cup raisins
- 1 dash sea salt
- few tablespoons water

Instructions:

1. Add all ingredients to a blender except the raisins and blend until smooth. Transfer to a bowl.
2. Fold in the raisins. Serve and enjoy.

WHOLE FOOD PLANT-BASED APPLE CRISP

Cook Time: 40 minutes

Servings: 8

Ingredients:

- 3/4 cup water
- 6 apples, sliced
- 1 tablespoon + 2 teaspoon cinnamon
- 1 tablespoon lemon juice
- 6 tablespoon maple syrup
- 1 1/2 cups oats
- 1 cup walnuts
- A pinch sea salt

Instructions:

1. Preheat the oven to 350F.
2. Mix water, lemon juice, 2 teaspoons cinnamon, 2 tablespoon maple syrup and dash sea salt in a bowl and pour over the apples in a dish.
3. Microwave the apple mixture on high for 5 minutes. Blend 1 cup oats until coarse. Add the remaining ingredients and blend until mixed well.
4. Add the crumbled mixture over the apples and bake for 40 minutes.

5. Serve and enjoy.

VEGAN CHOCOLATE BEET CAKE

Cook Time: 1 hour 20 minutes

Servings: 10

Ingredients:

- 1 cup coconut oil
- 1/2 cup semisweet chocolate chips
- 1 cup sugar
- 2 cups cooked beets, pureed
- 3 flax eggs
- 2 teaspoons baking soda
- 2 cups all-purpose flour
- 2 teaspoons vanilla
- 1/4 teaspoon salt

Instructions:

1. Preheat the oven to 375F.
2. Melt 1/4 cup coconut oil and chocolate chips over boiling water. Mix flax eggs and sugar in a bowl until combined well. Add beets, remaining coconut oil, vanilla and chocolate mixture.
3. Add baking soda, flour and salt in the beet mixture and combine well — transfer mixture to a greased Bundt pan and bake for 1 hour.
4. Remove from the oven, let cool and serve.

VEGAN BLUEBERRY FLAX MUFFINS

Cook Time: 50 minutes

Servings: 12

Ingredients:

- 1/4 cup ground flax
- 2 cups oat flour
- 2 teaspoons baking powder
- 1 teaspoon vanilla extract
- 4 tablespoons coconut oil, melted
- 1 teaspoon vinegar
- 1 cup almond milk
- 1/2 cup brown sugar
- 1/2 cup applesauce
- 1 1/2 cups blueberries
- 1/3 cup maple syrup
- 1/4 teaspoon salt

Instructions:

1. Preheat the oven to 375 F.
2. Mix vinegar and almond milk in a bowl and let rest for 10 minutes. Mix flaxseed, flour, salt, baking powder and cinnamon in a bowl and combine well.
3. Add coconut oil, applesauce, sugar and almond milk and vinegar mixture to the flour. Mix gently and fold in the blueberries.

4. Grease a muffin tray. Fill each of 12 tins with 3/4 way with batter. Bake for 30 minutes. Serve and enjoy.

CRANBERRY APPLE CIDER PIE

Cook time: 60 minutes

Servings: 6-8

Ingredients:

- 1/2 cup tap water
- 2 cups cranberries
- 1 orange zest and juice
- 1/3 cup maple syrup
- 1/3 cup sugar
- 4 cups apples, peeled and sliced
- 3/4 teaspoon cinnamon
- 1/2 teaspoon pumpkin pie spice
- 2 cups + 1 1/2 tablespoons all-purpose flour

- 1 1/4 teaspoon salt
- 2 2/3 tablespoons vegan butter
- 6 tablespoons of ice water

Instructions:

1. Preheat the oven to 400F. Mix tap water, maple syrup, and cranberries in a pan. Bring to a boil, then reduce heat to medium-low and stir for 10 minutes. Remove from heat and add orange juice and zest. Let cool.

2. Peel and slice apples into pieces. Mix with 1/3 cup sugar, 1/4 teaspoon salt, 1/2 teaspoon cinnamon, 1/4 teaspoon pumpkin pie spice, and 1 1/2 tablespoons flour.

3. Whisk the remaining flour, salt, cinnamon and pumpkin pie spice in a bowl. Add butter and mix until crumbly. Add ice water and mix well until the dough forms. Shape the dough into 2 balls, one bigger than other ones.

4. Roll the bigger ball into the crust and place it on a pie pan. Mix cranberry sauce and apple filling and add to the pan with the dough.

5. Roll out the other dough ball. Cut the crust into strips and make a top. Press down the edges and sprinkle with sugar and cinnamon.

6. Bake for 45 minutes. Let cool completely.

7. Serve and enjoy.

VEGAN CHOCOLATE AVOCADO PUDDING

Cook Time: 20 minutes

Servings: 6

Ingredients:

- 1 large banana
- 1 1/2 avocados
- 1/4 cup any sweetener
- 1/2 cup cacao powder
- 1/4 cup almond milk, unsweetened
- mixed berries for topping

Instructions:

1. Add all ingredients to a blender and blend until fully combined and smooth.
2. Transfer to a bowl, add toppings and serve.

LENTIL ROAST WITH BALSAMIC ONION GRAVY

Cook time: 1 hour

Servings: 6

Ingredients:

- 3 tablespoon vegetable oil
- 3 garlic cloves, minced
- 1 onion, minced
- 2 Portobello mushrooms, chopped
- 1 carrot, grated
- 4 tablespoons tamari soy sauce
- 2 tablespoons mixed dry herbs
- 4 tablespoons yeast
- 14 oz cooked kidney beans, rinsed
- 14 oz cooked puy lentils, rinsed
- 1 1/3 cup rolled oats
- 1 vegetable stock cube
- 1 red onion, sliced
- 1 tablespoon coconut sugar
- 1 tablespoon arrowroot powder
- 3 tablespoons balsamic vinegar
- 1 cup red wine
- black pepper, to taste

Instructions:

1. Preheat the oven to 350F and prepare a lined loaf tin.
2. Heat 1 tablespoon vegetable oil in a pan and cook onion and garlic until soft. Add carrot and mushroom and cook for 5 minutes more.
3. Add kidney beans, puy lentils, 1 tablespoon tamari sauce, herbs, yeast, oats, and little pepper and mash to combine. Transfer to the loaf tin and bake for 45 minutes.
4. Add 1/2 liter of vegetable stock with a stock cube and set aside. Add 2 tablespoons vegetable oil to a pan and add onion and coconut sugar and cook for 10 minutes.
5. Add arrowroot powder and stir to combine. Add balsamic vinegar, wine and tamari sauce and cook until stock is reduced. Add vegetable stock and cook for 10 minutes.
6. Serve with the bread loaf.

GRILLED BREADED TOFU STEAKS WITH SPINACH SALAD

Cook time: 25 minutes

Servings: 2

Ingredients:

- 1/2 block firm tofu
- 1 teaspoon tomato paste
- 1 tablespoon soy sauce
- 1 teaspoon miso paste
- 1 teaspoon sesame oil
- 1/4 cup breadcrumbs, 1/2 teaspoon maple syrup
- 2 cups baby spinach
- 1 tablespoon olive oil

- 1 tablespoon lemon juice
- 1 tablespoon pine nuts
- Salt and pepper, to taste

Instructions:

1. Add spinach, olive oil, lemon juice, pine nuts and salt and pepper to a bowl and toss well to make the spinach salad. Set aside. Squeeze water out of the tofu. Cut the block into 3 layers and slice across to make 6 triangles — drain water. Pat dry the tofu to remove excess water. Mix tomato paste, soy sauce, miso paste, maple syrup and sesame oil in a bowl and mix well to combine. Add breadcrumbs to a separate dish. Dip tofu steaks in the sauce and coat with breadcrumbs repeat with every piece. Grease a ribbed grill pan. Preheat the grill to medium-high and cook tofu steaks for 13 minutes, flip over and cook for 10 minutes on another side. Serve and enjoy.

SWEET POTATO AND BLACK BEAN ENCHILADAS

Cook Time: 70 minutes

Servings: 5

Ingredients:

- 1 teaspoon olive oil
- 1 onion, diced
- 5 garlic cloves, minced
- 1 jalapeno, seeded and diced
- 10 oz. can diced tomatoes with green chilies
- 2 1/2 cups sweet potatoes, peeled and cut into 1/2" cubes
- 1 1/2 cups canned black beans, drained and rinsed
- 1/4 cup cilantro
- 1/2 teaspoon chili powder
- 1 1/2 teaspoon ground cumin
- 10 whole wheat flour tortillas
- 2 cups Mexican cheese, shredded
- 2 tablespoon vegetable oil
- 1 1/2 cups tomato sauce
- 1/2 teaspoon chipotle chili powder
- 3/4 cup chicken broth
- 3 chipotle chilies in adobo sauce
- Salt and black pepper, to taste

Instructions:

1. Preheat the oven to 400F. Spread 1/4 cup red enchilada sauce on the bottom of a baking dish.

2. Heat olive oil in a skillet over medium-high heat. Add onions, 3 garlic cloves and jalapeno and cook for 2 minutes.

3. Add diced tomatoes, cubed sweet tomatoes, cilantro, black beans, 1 teaspoon cumin, chili powder, 1/4 cup water and salt and pepper — cover and cook for 10 minutes over medium-low heat.

4. Add 1/3 cup filling in the center of each tortilla, roll and place seam side down on the baking dish. Add 3/4 cup enchilada sauce and cheese over it. Cover with foil and bake for 10 minutes. Top with cilantro.

5. Add onion and garlic to the pan placed over medium-low heat and cook for 30 seconds. Add chicken broth, tomato sauce, chili powder, cumin, chipotle chilies and salt and pepper. Bring to boil. Reduce the heat and cook for 7 minutes.

6. Serve enchiladas with sauce.

EDAMAME FRIED RICE

Cook Time: 15 minutes

Servings: 4

Ingredients:

- 3 tablespoon vegetable oil
- 1 red bell pepper, diced
- 4 scallions, sliced, white and green parts separated
- 2 garlic cloves, chopped
- 1 cup shelled edamame
- 2 eggs
- 2 cups long-grain white rice, cooked
- 2 tablespoon soy sauce

Instructions:

1. Heat oil in a skillet over medium heat. Add bell peppers and scallion whites and cook for about 3-4 minutes. Add garlic and edamame and cook for 30 seconds more.

2. Crack the eggs into the skillet and fry until cooked and scrambled. Add soy sauce. Add rice and stir well to combine.

3. Top with scallion greens and serve.

VEGAN SHEPHERD'S PIE WITH CRISPY CAULIFLOWER CRUST

Cook Time: 1 hour 20 minutes

Servings: 4

Ingredients:

- 1 tablespoon coconut oil
- 3/4 cup brown lentils, uncooked
- 2 celery stalks, diced
- 2 cups savoy cabbage, chopped
- 1 carrot, diced
- 1 cup of water
- 1 garlic clove, minced
- 1 tablespoon balsamic vinegar
- 1 tablespoon vegan Worcestershire sauce
- 1 tablespoon tomato paste
- 1/8 teaspoon ground cloves
- 2 tablespoon olive oil
- 1/2 head cauliflower, chopped
- 1 teaspoon salt
- black pepper, to taste

Instructions:

1. Preheat the oven to 375F.

2. Add lentils to a pan and cover with water. Bring to a boil, reduce the heat to medium and cook for about 30 minutes. Drain and set aside.

3. Steam cauliflower until tender. Add to a blender with olive oil, 1/2 teaspoon salt, pepper and blend until smooth.

4. Heat coconut oil in a skillet over medium heat. Add celery, carrot, cabbage, and garlic. Cook for about 8 minutes. Add reserved cooked lentils, vinegar, water, Worcestershire, tomato paste, cloves, salt, and pepper.

5. Pour the filling mixture into a ceramic baking dish. Add dollops of cauliflower crust on top and spread evenly. Bake for about 30 minutes serve and enjoy!

HEARTY VEGETARIAN CHILI WITH BUTTERNUT SQUASH

Cook Time: 1 hour 35 minutes

Servings: 6

Ingredients:

- 8 oz. Yukon Gold potatoes, peeled and chopped
- 2 cups vegetable broth
- 2 tablespoon olive oil
- 1 onion, chopped
- 1 poblano chile pepper, seeded and chopped
- 3 tablespoon lime juice
- 1 tablespoon Worcestershire sauce
- 1 carrot, chopped

- 1 ribs celery, chopped
- 1 jalapeno, seeded and diced
- 4 garlic cloves, minced
- 1 teaspoon dried oregano
- 2 cans whole tomatillos, drained and chopped
- 1 butternut squash, peeled and chopped
- 1 can white beans, drained and rinsed
- 1 can pinto beans, drained and rinsed
- 1/2 cup frozen corn, thawed
- 1/4 cup cilantro, chopped
- 1 tablespoon chili powder
- 1 tablespoon paprika
- 1 teaspoon ground cumin
- 1 teaspoon salt
- 1/2 teaspoon pepper
- sour cream
- lime wedges
- tortilla chips

Instructions:

1. Heat oil in a pan over medium heat. Add poblano, onions, carrot, celery, garlic, chili powder, jalapeno, cumin, oregano, paprika, salt, and pepper. Cook for about 10 minutes, stirring often.

2. Add broth, tomatillos, and Worcestershire sauce and bring everything to a boil. Add potatoes, butternut squash, pinto beans, and white beans — Cook for about 1 hour.

3. Add cilantro, lime juice, and corn — Cook for 2 minutes.

4. Serve with sour cream, tortilla chips, and lime wedges.

EASY BANANA-CACAO ICE CREAM

Cook Time: 5 minutes + freezing

Servings: 4

Ingredients:

- 1 tablespoon raw cacao powder
- 2 bananas, frozen
- 1 teaspoon maca powder
- 1 teaspoon maple syrup
- 2 teaspoons natural peanut butter
- 1 scoop vegan chocolate protein powder
- pinch cinnamon
- splash almond milk
- chia seeds
- ground flax seeds
- almonds, chopped
- cacao nibs

Instructions:

1. Blend the first 8 ingredients in a blender on high speed.
2. Transfer the mixture to a container and place it into the freezer. Freeze for about 4-8 hours, stirring every 1 hour
3. Serve topped with cacao nibs, ground flax seeds, chia seeds, and almonds.

FLOURLESS WALNUT KIDNEY BEAN BROWNIES

Cook Time: 30 minutes

Servings: 20

Ingredients:

- 1/2 cup cacao powder
- 14 oz. can kidney beans
- 1 teaspoon vanilla extract
- 1/8 cup natural date syrup
- 1/3 cup coconut sugar
- 1 teaspoon baking powder
- 2 flax eggs
- 1/4 cup coconut oil, melted
- 1/3 cup walnut pieces
- pinch Himalayan salt

Instructions:

1. Preheat the oven to 345 F and drain and rinse kidney beans.
2. Add the beans and the remaining ingredients into a blender and process well until smooth. Line a brownie dish with parchment paper and add the butter to it. Spread evenly.
3. Bake for 30 minutes, remove and let cool. Cut into squares and serve.

RAW PROTEIN THIN MINTS

Cook Time: 5 minutes

Servings: 10 cookies

Ingredients:

- 2 1/2 tablespoons cocoa
- 1 teaspoon vanilla extract
- 3/4 cup protein powder
- 1/2 teaspoon stevia, liquid
- 7 tablespoons coconut oil, melted
- 1 teaspoon peppermint extract

Instructions:

1. Add all ingredients to a bowl and mix well to combine. Transfer to a tray and refrigerate.
2. Store in a freezer until hard to touch. Serve.

FUDGY CINNAMON CHAI PROTEIN BARS

Cook time: 10 minutes + chilling time

Servings: 6

Ingredients:

- 6 dates, soaked in 1/4 cup boiling water
- 15 oz. can chickpeas, drained and rinsed
- 1 teaspoon bourbon vanilla
- 1 tablespoon chai tea leaves infused in boiling water with dates
- 2 1/2 tablespoons coconut oil
- 3/8 teaspoon stevia powder
- 2 1/2 tablespoon vegan vanilla protein powder
- 1 1/2 teaspoons cinnamon
- 4 tablespoons coconut flour

Instructions:

1. Mix soaked dates, chickpeas, vanilla, tea, coconut oil, cinnamon, stevia powder, and vanilla protein powder in a blender and blend until smooth.
2. Add coconut flour and blend until it thickens. Transfer to a loaf pan and place into a freezer.
3. Let sit until firm then transfer to the fridge 30 minutes before serving.
4. Slice into squares and serve.

ROSEMARY FIG SCONES

Cook Time: 40 minutes

Servings: 8

Ingredients:

- 1/4 cup coconut sugar
- 2 cups brown rice flour
- 1/2 cup coconut oil, cold
- 1 tablespoon baking powder
- 1 cup non-dairy milk
- 3 tablespoons rosemary, chopped
- 1 tablespoon lemon zest

- 1/2 cup dry figs, chopped
- 1/4 teaspoon salt

Instructions:

1. Preheat the oven to 350F.

2. Mix rosemary, lemon zest and milk in a bowl and set aside.

3. Mix coconut sugar, brown rice flour, baking powder, coconut oil and salt in a bowl. Add coconut oil into the flour mixture and stir to combine. Add dried figs into it.

4. Mix dry and wet ingredients and make the dough. Roll out the dough into a circle about 1 1/2" thick. Cut the dough into 8 pieces.

5. Transfer the pieces to a parchment-lined baking sheet and bake for 18 minutes.

6. Serve and enjoy.

CARROT CAKE WAFFLES

Cook Time: 15 minutes

Servings: 4

Ingredients:

- 1 cup flour, gluten-free
- 2 tablespoons coconut sugar
- 1/2 teaspoon cinnamon
- 1 teaspoon baking powder
- 1 1/2 tablespoons ground flax seeds
- 3/4 cup almond milk
- 1 teaspoon apple cider vinegar
- 1/2 cup carrots, grated
- 2 1/2 tablespoons warm water
- 1/4 cup pineapple, crushed
- 2 tablespoon coconut flakes
- 1 pinch ground ginger
- 1 pinch salt

Instructions:

1. Preheat waffle iron. Mix almond milk and vinegar in a bowl. Add warm water to the flax seeds to make the flax egg.

2. Mix the dry ingredients and combine well. Add almond milk mixture, coconut, and crushed pineapple to it and mix.

3. Add the grated carrots and flax egg. Scoop the batter into the waffle iron and cook until crispy and golden.

4. Serve and enjoy.

HIGH PROTEIN DESSERT PIZZA WITH RASPBERRY SAUCE

Cook Time: 30 minutes

Servings: 4

Ingredients:

- 1/4 cup chickpea flour
- 1/4 cup cacao powder
- 1 packet Plant Fusion Lean Chocolate Brownie Flavor
- 3 tablespoons maple syrup
- 2 tablespoons coconut oil
- 1/2 teaspoon vanilla extract
- 1 cup coconut cream
- 1 lemon, zested
- 12 oz. raspberries
- 1 tablespoon lemon juice

Instructions:

1. Preheat the oven to 350F. Mix Plant Fusion Lean, chickpea flour and cacao powder in a bowl. Mix 2 tablespoons maple syrup and coconut oil. Add to the dry ingredients and mix until smooth.

2. Roll out the dough into a circle. Place onto a parchment paper. Bake for 14 minutes and let cool. Mix raspberries, lemon zest, and juice in a pot. Bring to a boil and cook until jam-like consistency forms and let cool.

3. Beat coconut milk in a bowl on high for 2 minutes. Add vanilla extract and maple syrup and beat until well mixed. Cut the pizza crust into 8 pieces, top with raspberries, raspberry jam and coconut cream and serve.

HIGH PROTEIN, RAW VEGAN CARROT CAKE

Cook time: 5 minutes

Servings: 4

Ingredients:

- 1/2 cup dried coconut
- 2 carrots
- 1/2 cup ground almonds
- 2 tablespoon orange zest
- 2 tablespoon orange juice
- 1 teaspoon cinnamon
- 2 teaspoon stevia
- 1/4 teaspoon ground nutmeg
- 1/2 cup pecans
- 3 tablespoon vanilla protein powder
- 2 tablespoons lemon juice
- 2 cups soaked cashews
- 2 tablespoon maple syrup
- 2 tablespoon coconut oil
- Water

Instructions:

1. Blend the first 10 ingredients in a blender until smooth. Add the blended mix to a cake pan. Bake for about 45-50 minutes.

2. Blend the remaining ingredients in a blender until smooth. Add water if needed.

3. Add frosting over cake and serve.

HIGH PROTEIN RICE CRISPIE TREATS

Cook Time: 10 minutes

Servings: 8 treats

Ingredients:

- 1/4 cup vanilla plant-based protein powder
- 2 cups crisp rice cereal
- 3 tablespoons brown rice syrup
- 3 tablespoons creamy nut butter

Instructions:

1. Grease an 8 cup muffin tin. Mix protein powder and cereal in a bowl.

2. Heat a pan over medium heat. Cook the syrup and nut butter until mixtures start bubbling. Cook for 30 seconds longer.

3. Add over cereal mixture and stir well. Add to the prepared muffin cups. Press it down into the bottom of the cups.

4. Cool completely, remove and serve.